BOOK 4

Palmer-Hughes
ACCORDION COURSE
by Bill Palmer and Bill Hughes

This book belongs to_____

My teacher is_____

I began this book_____

ALFRED PUBLISHING CO., INC.
All rights reserved.   Printed in USA.

FOREWORD

• • •

Book 4 of the PALMER-HUGHES ACCORDION COURSE is principally concerned with the following problems:

1. Introducing and using 3 new **COUNTERBASSES**.

2. Introducing all the **SHARP MAJOR KEYS**, with special emphasis on the key of **D MAJOR**.

3. Introducing the **UPPER LEGER LINES** of the **TREBLE STAFF**, and developing skill in reading the **UPPER** and **LOWER LEGER LINES**.

4. Introducing **GRACE NOTES** and **TRILLS**.

THE STUDENT WHO GAINS SUFFICIENT EXPERIENCE IN PLAYING IN THE KEY OF D MAJOR WILL HAVE LITTLE DIFFICULTY WHEN THE KEY OF A MAJOR IS INTRODUCED IN BOOK 5, AND WILL NEVER REGARD THE SHARP KEYS AS DIFFICULT KEYS.

the publishers

• • •

CHORD STUDY is introduced in a separate book, the PALMER-HUGHES CHORD BOOK. This enables the teacher to adapt the presentation of this material to the varying abilities, temperaments and desires of different students.

CONTENTS

THEMES FROM
SECOND HUNGARIAN RHAPSODY

FRANZ LISZT

Allegro

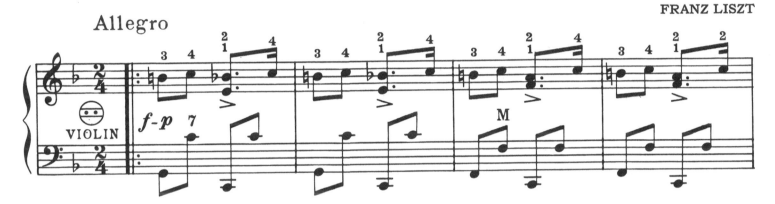

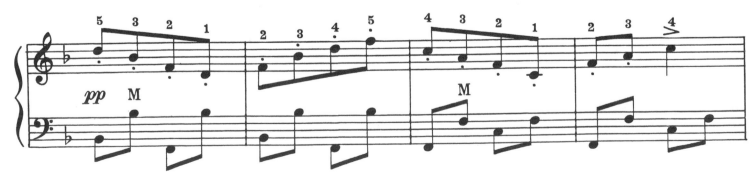

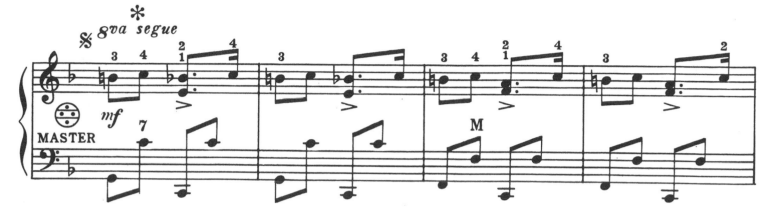

* SEGUE—Continue in the same manner. (In this case continue to play 8va.)

5

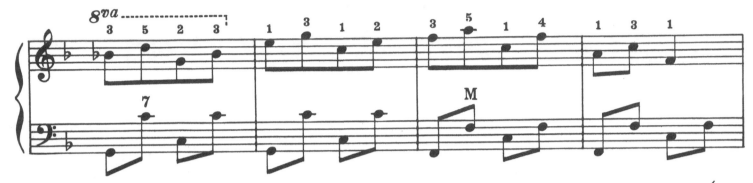

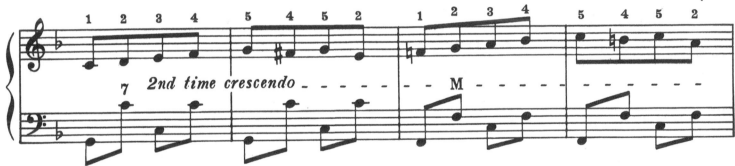

Presto *(very fast)*

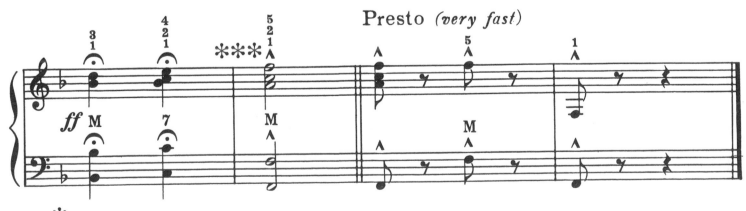

* *LOCO*— (Location). As written (not 8va).

** *D.S.* —Abbreviation for "Dal Segno," meaning "From the Sign." REPEAT from the SIGN (𝄋).

*** ∧ ——A very heavy accent, stronger than indicated by >.

MORE MAJOR SCALES

THE C MAJOR SCALE:

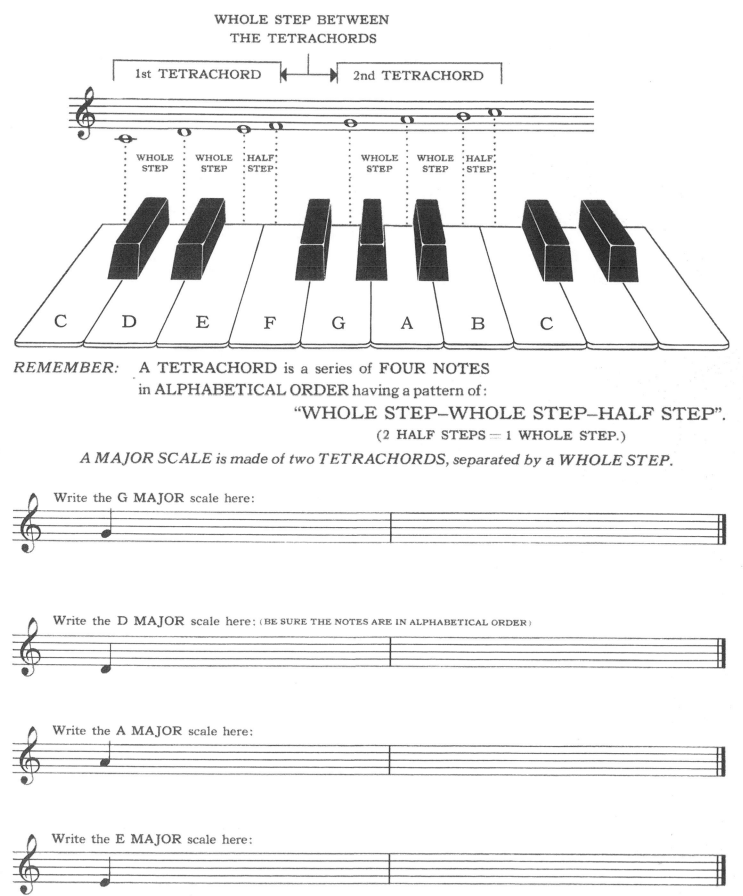

WHOLE STEP BETWEEN
THE TETRACHORDS

1st TETRACHORD · 2nd TETRACHORD

WHOLE STEP · WHOLE STEP · HALF STEP · WHOLE STEP · WHOLE STEP · HALF STEP

C D E F G A B C

REMEMBER: A TETRACHORD is a series of FOUR NOTES
in ALPHABETICAL ORDER having a pattern of:

"WHOLE STEP–WHOLE STEP–HALF STEP".

(2 HALF STEPS — 1 WHOLE STEP.)

A MAJOR SCALE is made of two TETRACHORDS, separated by a WHOLE STEP.

Write the G MAJOR scale here:

Write the D MAJOR scale here: (BE SURE THE NOTES ARE IN ALPHABETICAL ORDER)

Write the A MAJOR scale here:

Write the E MAJOR scale here:

NEW COUNTERBASSES

REMEMBER, any counterbass is THREE SCALE TONES higher than the corresponding FUNDAMENTAL BASS. Since the third tone of the scales of D, A and E are SHARP, the counterbasses of these three notes are also SHARP!

F# is the COUNTERBASS of D:

C# is the COUNTERBASS of A:

G# is the COUNTERBASS of E:

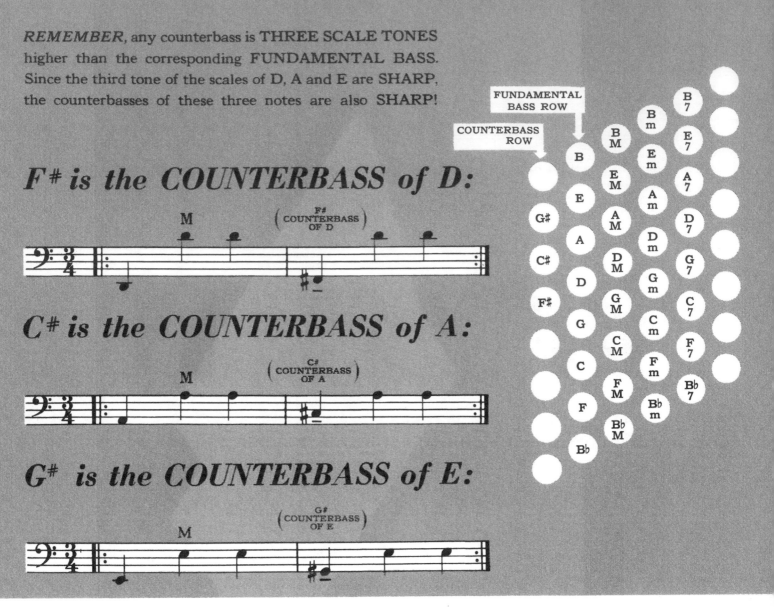

Preparation for "A-HUNTING WE WILL GO"

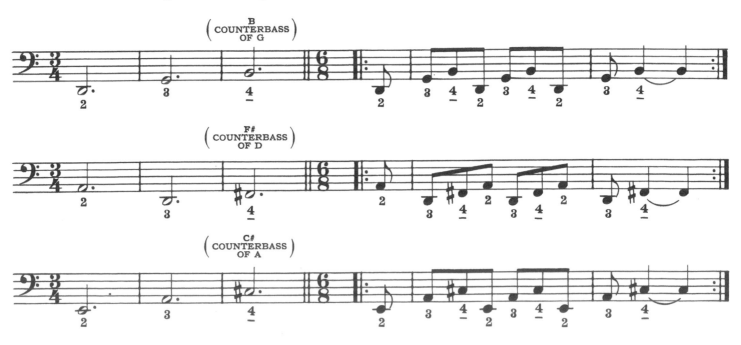

A-HUNTING WE WILL GO!

Adapted from traditional melodies
by PALMER-HUGHES

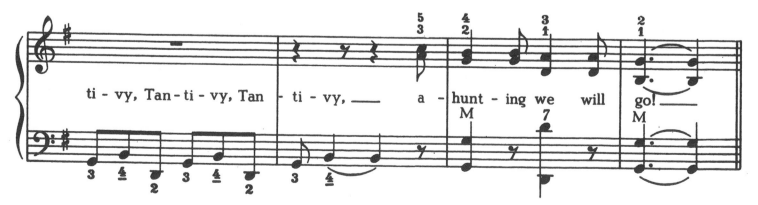

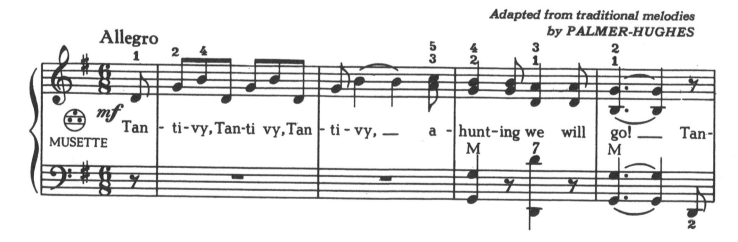

A - hunt-ing we will go,___ a - hunt-ing we will go,___ a -

hunt - ing we will go,___ a - hunt-ing we will go!___

MASTER

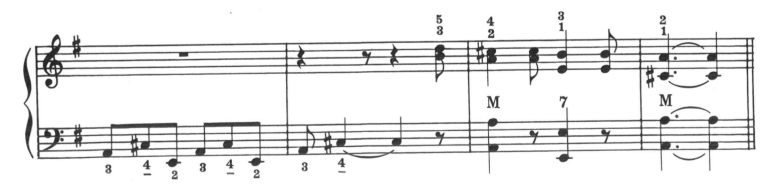

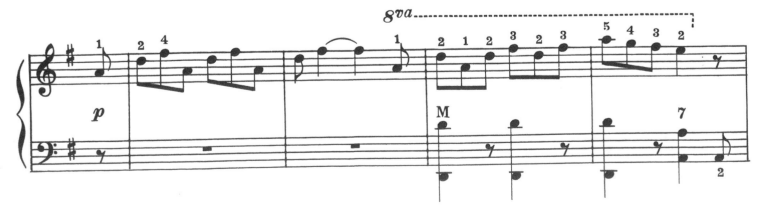

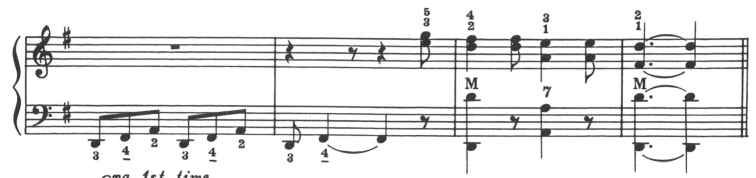

8va 1st time
loco 2nd time

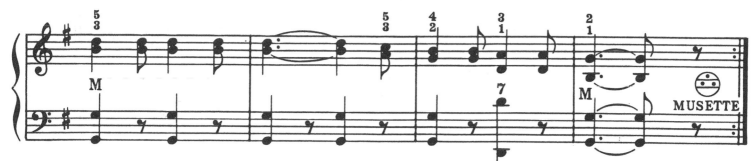

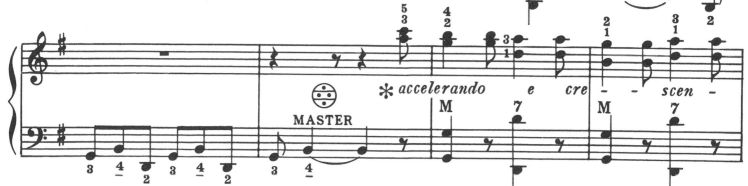

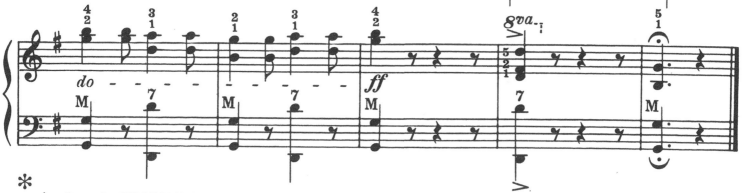

*

Accelerando: GRADUALLY FASTER.

11

SPEED DRILL No. 8

PRACTICE LEGATO AND STACCATO:

TEMPO MARKS

The following **TEMPO MARKS** are used in Book 4. Some of these have already been used in Book 3, but are listed here for the purpose of review. You may refer to this page for their meanings, but they must be memorized before this book is finished.

MODERATO—Moderately
ALLEGRO—Lively, fast
PRESTO—Very fast
ACCELERANDO—Gradually faster

RITARDANDO—Gradually slower
A TEMPO—Resume original speed
TEMPO di MARCIA—March Tempo
TEMPO di VALSE—Waltz Tempo

Several of these words may be combined. For example: *ALLEGRO MODERATO*—Moderately fast.

THE G MAJOR SCALE FOR LEFT HAND

Notice that the **G MAJOR SCALE** has exactly the same fingering as the **C MAJOR SCALE**.

ALL MAJOR SCALES FOR THE LEFT HAND HAVE THE SAME FINGERING.

THE STAR SPANGLED BANNER

With spirit

KEY-SMITH

REPEATED NOTE EXERCISE

PREPARATION FOR "LIGHT CAVALRY OVERTURE"

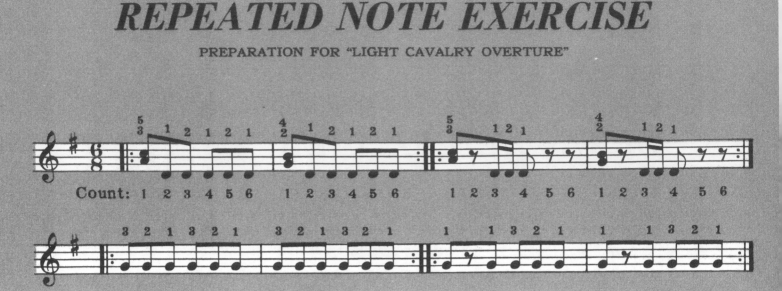

Count: 1 2 3 4 5 6   1 2 3 4 5 6   1 2 3 4 5 6   1 2 3 4 5 6

LIGHT CAVALRY

2nd time 8va segue

SUPPE

Allegro

14

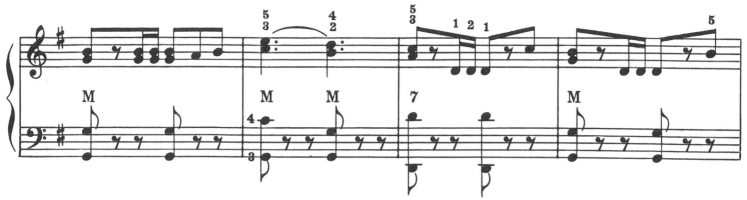

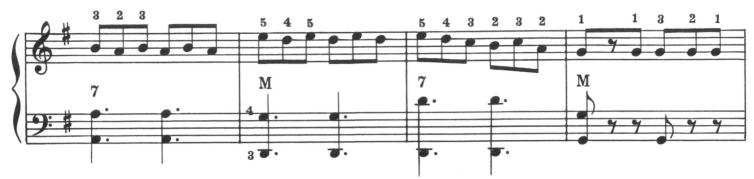

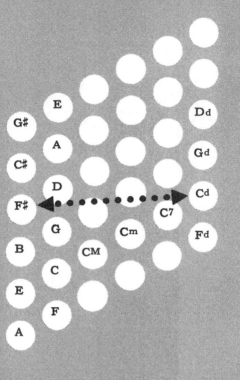

THE DIMINISHED CHORD WITH THE COUNTERBASS

The diminished chord is very commonly used with the counterbass of the note that is one full tone above the fundamental of the chord. The third finger plays the counterbass, the second finger plays the diminished chord. This stretch may seem difficult at first, but it is easily mastered with a little practice. Notice that the stretch is actually a straight line across the keyboard, and is therefore the shortest distance from any counterbass button to any diminished chord button.

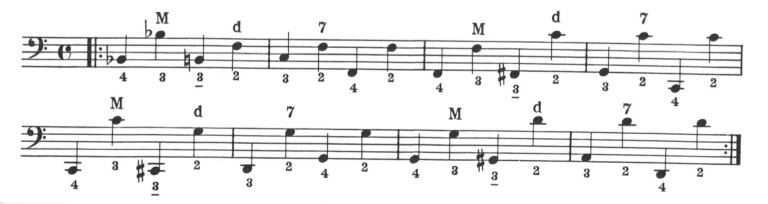

Preparation for "YOU TELL ME YOUR DREAM"

YOU TELL ME YOUR DREAM

DANIELS

Tempo di valse

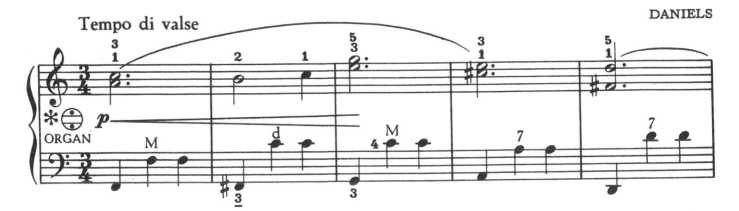

✳ ⊖ BANDONEON MAY BE SUBSTITUTED

18

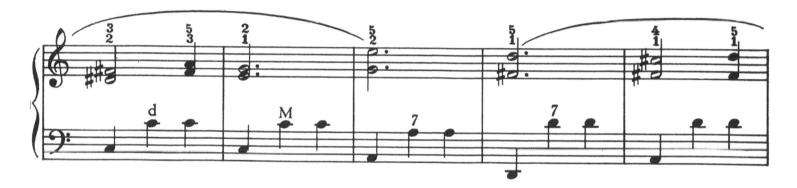

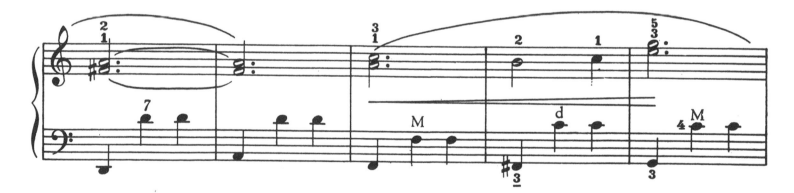

SPEED DRILL No. 9

PRACTICE LEGATO AND STACCATO:

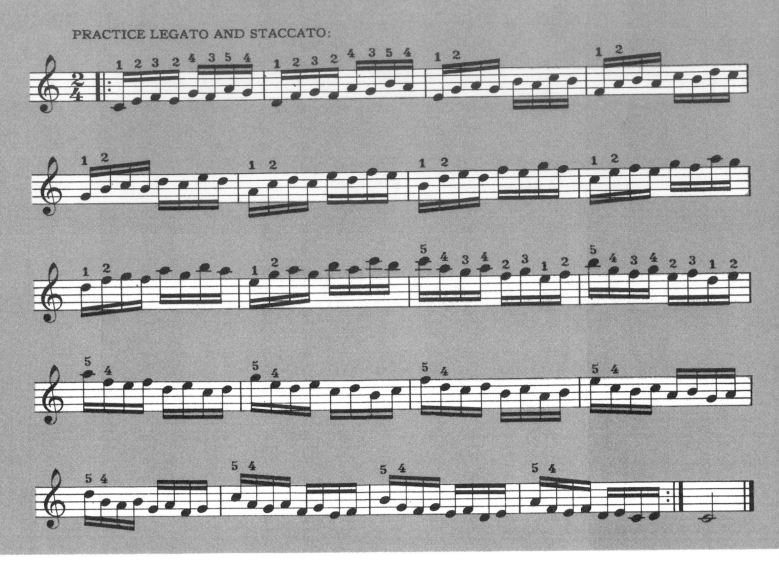

THE KEY OF D MAJOR

Practice this scale DAILY, legato and staccato.

THE D MAJOR SCALE FOR RIGHT HAND:

THE D MAJOR SCALE FOR LEFT HAND:

IMPORTANT! Practice SPEED DRILL No. 8 in the key of D MAJOR. To do this change the key signature to TWO SHARPS, and begin and end on D instead of C. The fingering remains the same.

COTTON-EYED JOE (SQUARE DANCE)

TRADITIONAL

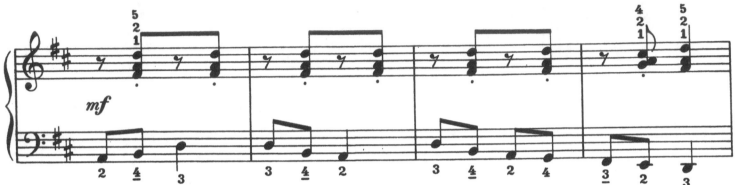

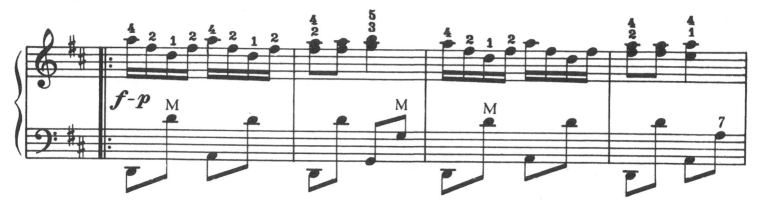

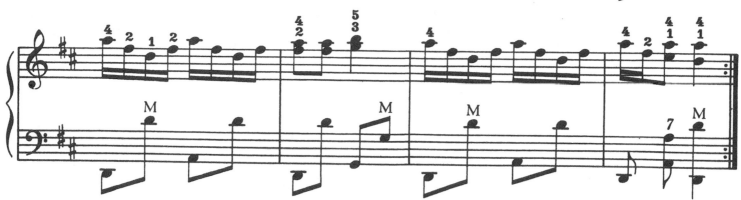

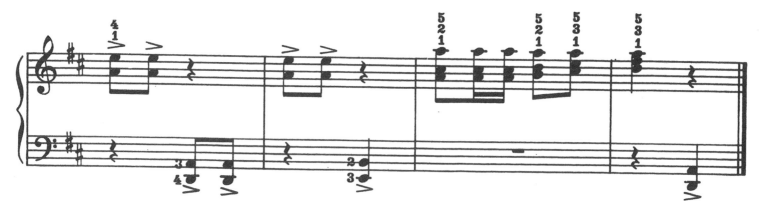

INTRODUCING THE UPPER
LEGER LINES OF THE TREBLE

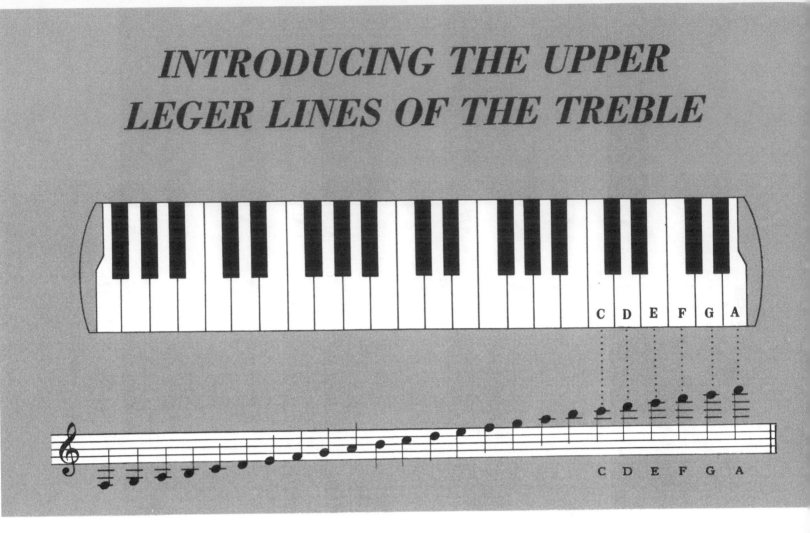

TWO OCTAVE D MAJOR SCALE

TWO OCTAVE F MAJOR SCALE

TWO OCTAVE G MAJOR SCALE

READING AND WRITING
UPPER LEGER LINES

WRITE THE LETTER NAME OF EACH NOTE IN THE SQUARE JUST BELOW IT:

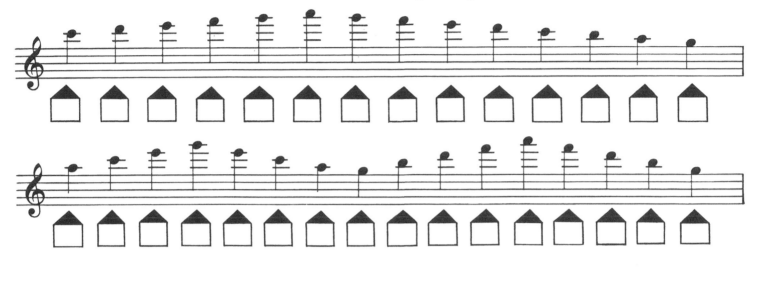

WRITE THE CORRECT NOTE UNDER EACH SQUARE. USE UPPER LEGER LINES ONLY!

| C | E | G | B | D | F | A | G | E | C | A | B | F | D |

| A | B | G | C | F | D | B | F | C | A | D | G | E | B |

SPELLING GAME

WRITE THE LETTER NAMES:

CIRIBIRIBIN

A. PESTALOZZA

Allegro Moderato

26

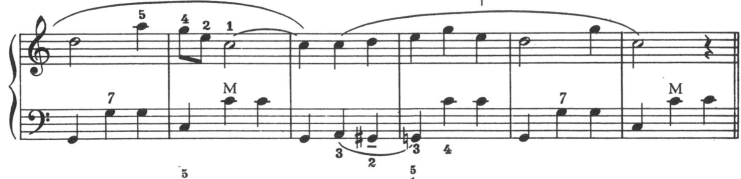

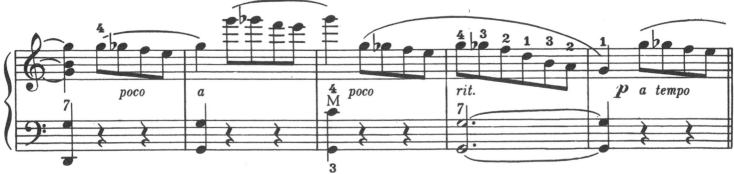

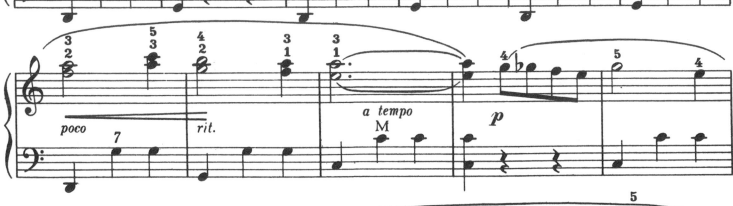

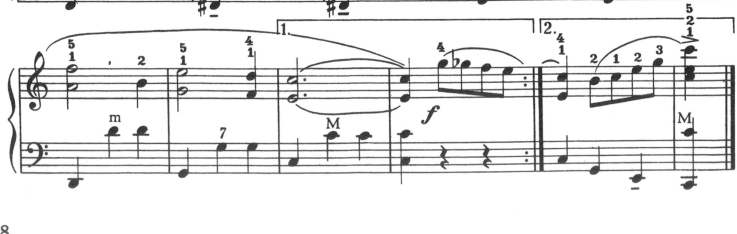

SPEED DRILL No. 10

PRACTICE LEGATO AND STACCATO:

INTRODUCING GRACE NOTES

THESE ARE GRACE NOTES:

GRACE NOTES of this type are always played very quickly, and should be thought of as belonging to the note that follows them.

AS WRITTEN:

GRACE NOTE STUDY

SCOTLAND, THE BRAVE

TRADITIONAL

* When written below the bass staff, these signs tell you which bass shifts to use. The first one is called **TENOR**. It tells you to use the shift that **CUTS OUT** the **LOW REED**. The second one is called **MASTER**. It tells you to use the shift that **CUTS IN** the **LOW REED**. When no **SHIFT MARK** appears below the bass staff, it is understood that the **MASTER SHIFT** is to be used.

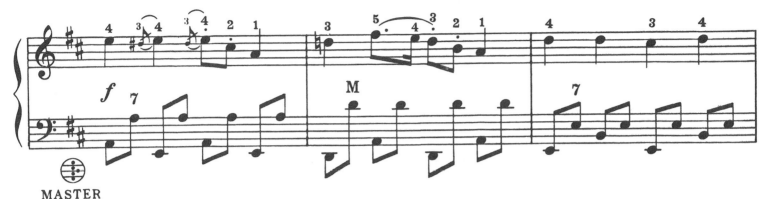

MASTER

MASTER

COUNTERBASS REVIEW

FILL IN THE BLANK STAVES:

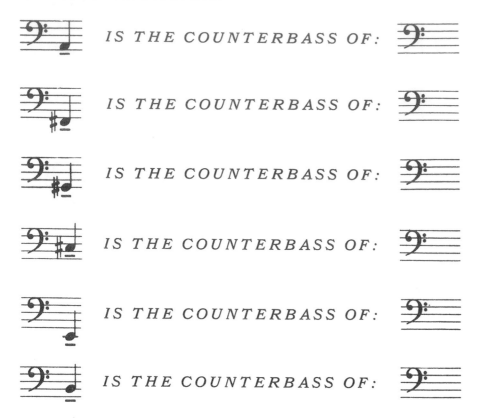

IS THE COUNTERBASS OF:

IS THE COUNTERBASS OF:

IS THE COUNTERBASS OF:

IS THE COUNTERBASS OF:

IS THE COUNTERBASS OF:

IS THE COUNTERBASS OF:

BASS EXERCISE

The MINOR CHORD is often used with a FUNDAMENTAL BASS the *THIRD ROW BELOW. The 5th finger MUST be used on the FUNDAMENTAL BASS when this pattern occurs.

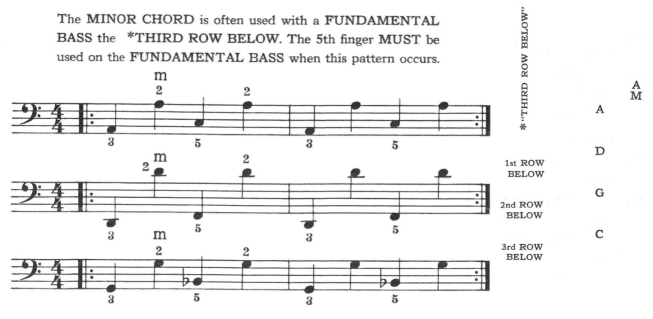

Preparation for "THE THUNDERER"

32

INTRODUCING THE TRILL

A TRILL IS PRODUCED BY RAPIDLY ALTERNATING THE WRITTEN NOTE WITH THE NEXT SCALE TONE.

PRACTICE THIS EXERCISE WITH THE FOLLOWING FINGER COMBINATIONS:
1 and 2, 2—3, 3—4, 4—5. START VERY SLOWLY, GRADUALLY INCREASING SPEED.

TRILL STUDY

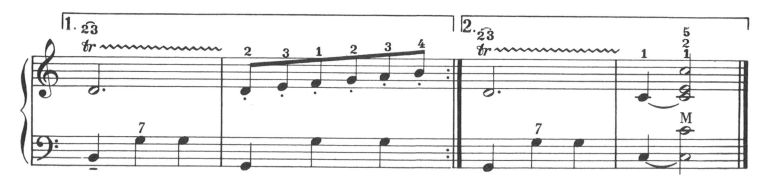

33

THE THUNDERER

SOUSA

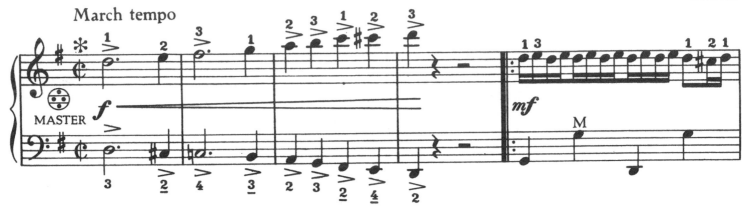

 *Alla Breve*, sometimes called "cut time." This indicates $\frac{2}{2}$ time. The relative time values of notes are the same as in $\frac{4}{4}$ time. In effect, it is a doubling of the tempo when compared to $\frac{4}{4}$ time, and the "beat" of the music is felt in twos rather than in fours.

34

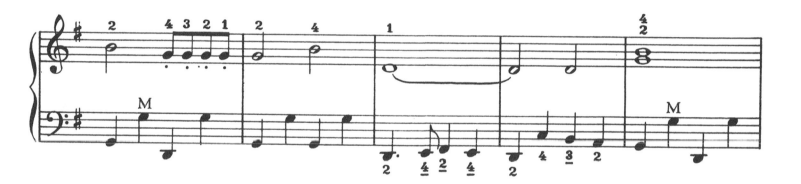

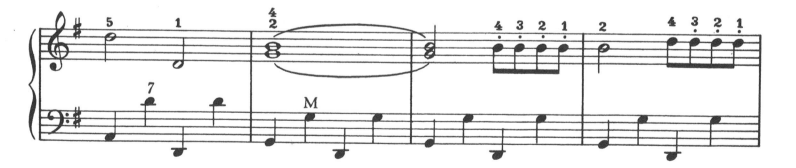

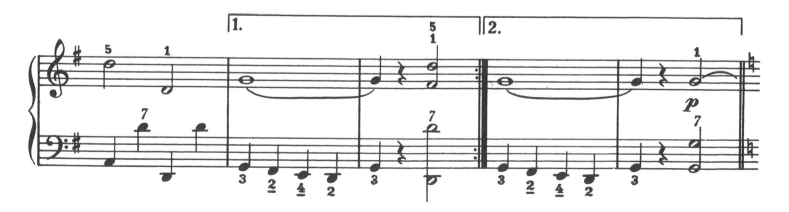

35

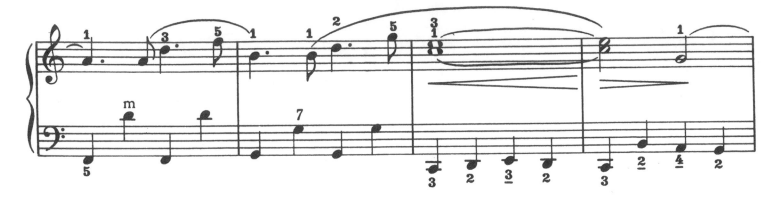

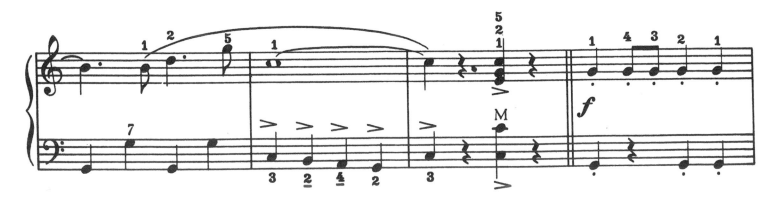

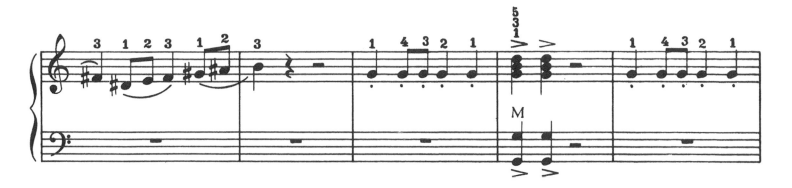

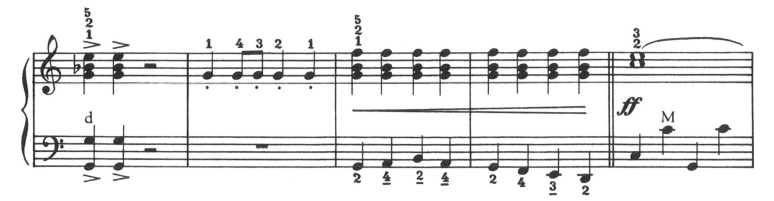

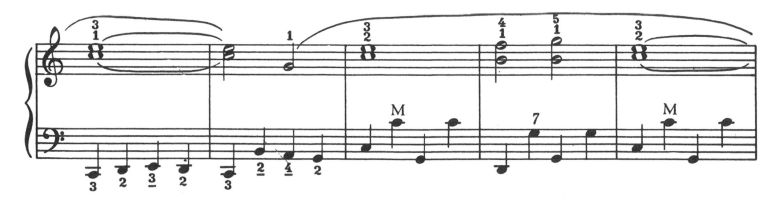

Jumping Beans

Solo or Duet

1st Accordion

PALMER-HUGHES

Moderato

1st time Moderato
2nd time Allegro
3rd time Presto

1st Accordion

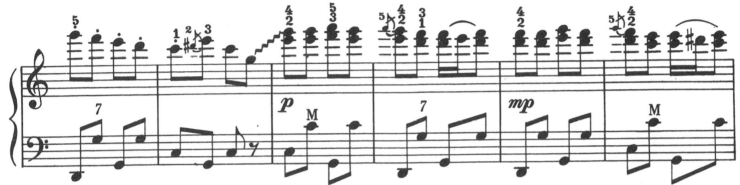

*LOCO — "location" — play as written (not 8va).

Jumping Beans

2nd Accordion

PALMER-HUGHES

Moderato

1st time Moderato
2nd time Allegro
3rd time Presto

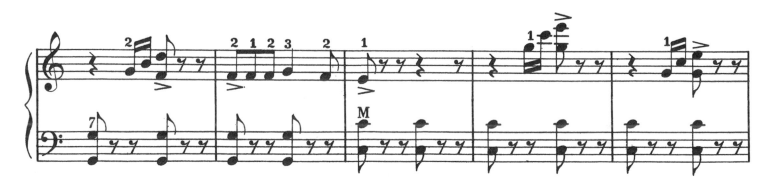

40

2nd Accordion

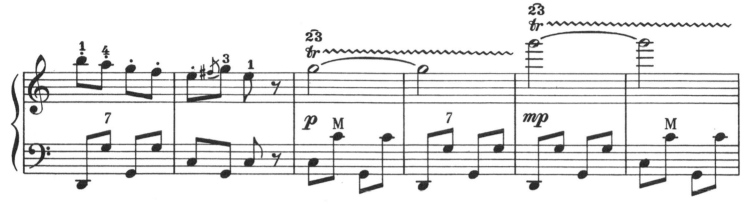

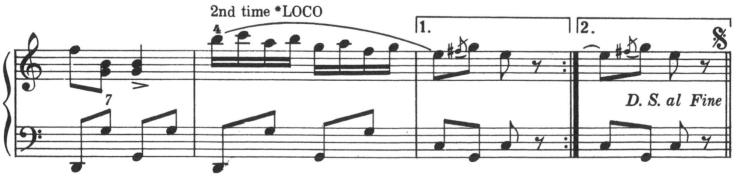

*LOCO — "location" — play as written (not 8va).

SPEED DRILL No. 11

PRACTICE LEGATO AND STACCATO:

REPEATED NOTE EXERCISES

Preparation for "COMEDIANS' DANCE"

1. START VERY SLOWLY. GRADUALLY INCREASE SPEED.
2. KEEP FINGERS VERY CLOSE TO KEYS.

MASTER THE FOLLOWING EXERCISE THOROUGHLY BEFORE PROCEEDING TO "COMEDIANS' DANCE":

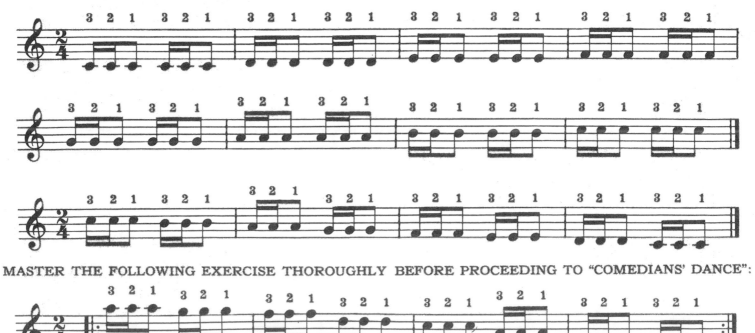

COMEDIANS' DANCE

Allegro

G. KABALEVSKY

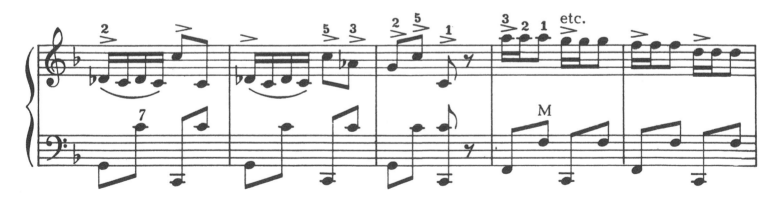

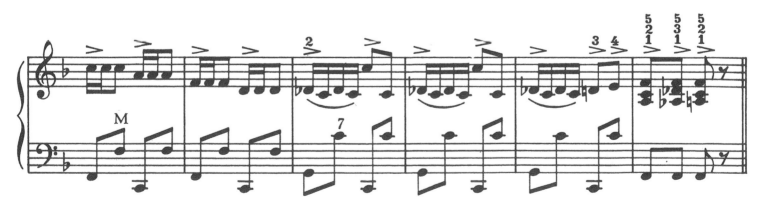

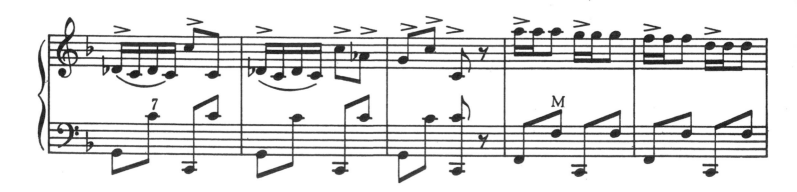

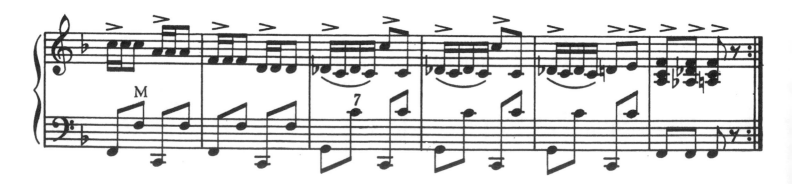

44

EXERCISES IN SYNCOPATION

THE EFFECT OF PLAYING ON THE "OFF BEAT" (AHEAD OF, OR BEHIND THE REGULAR BEAT) IS CALLED *SYNCOPATION*. THIS IS DEMONSTRATED IN THE SECOND LINE OF THE ABOVE EXERCISE.

A NEW STYLE OF BASS

Preparation for "LA CUCARACHA." This style of bass playing is also used often in marches and music of other types.

LA CUCARACHA

TRADITIONAL

Place a T in front of each TRUE statement
and an F in front of each FALSE statement:

——— 1. PRESTO means "very fast."

——— 2. The key of E Major has FIVE SHARPS.

——— 3. SYNCOPATION is playing on the "off beat."

——— 4. LOCO means "gradually faster."

——— 5. D.S. means "repeat from the sign (𝄋)."

——— 6. D.C. means "repeat from the BEGINNING."

——— 7. The two sharps of the key of D Major are F♯ and C♯.

——— 8. SEGUE means "continue in the same manner."

——— 9. All major scales for the left hand have the same fingering.

——— 10. All major scales for the right hand have the same fingering.

——— 11. A trill is produced by alternating the written note with the next black note.

——— 12. Grace notes are always written smaller than ordinary notes.

——— 13. The key of F Major has SIX SHARPS.

——— 14. A TEMPO means "gradually slower."

——— 15. ALLEGRO MODERATO means "moderately slow."

——— 16. ACCELERANDO means "gradually faster."

——— 17. The counterbass of E is G♯.

——— 18. The counterbass of A is C♯.

——— 19. D is the counterbass of F♯.

——— 20. F♯ is the counterbass of D.

SCORE 5 POINTS FOR EACH CORRECT
ANSWER. PASSING GRADE IS 80.

GRADE_____